Friend & Lover

Books by JOHN DITSKY

POETRY

The Katherine Poems
Scar Tissue
Friend & Lover

CRITICISM

Essays on East of Eden
The Onstage Christ

ONTARIO REVIEW PRESS
POETRY SERIES

Friend & Lover

Poems by JOHN DITSKY

THE ONTARIO REVIEW PRESS
Princeton, New Jersey

Poems here were first published in or accepted for:
*Agni Review, The Alchemist, ARC, Aspen Leaves, The
Blue Fife, Canadian Literature, The Carleton Miscellany,
College English, Concerning Poetry, Corridors, Crop
Dust, C.S.P. World News, The Dalhousie Review, Descant,
Fifth Sun, Gray Sky Review, The Hollins Critic, Image,
Iron, Italia*America, The Literary Review, The Malahat
Review, The Midatlantic Review, Modern Poetry Studies,
Nebula, New Collage, NeWest ReView, Nimrod, Nitty-Gritty,
Nocturne, The Old Red Kimono, The Ontario Review, Other
Voices, Palantir, Panache, Proteus, The Remington Review,
Review Ottawa, Samphire, Seven Stars, Southern Humanities
Review, Syncline, Velvet Wings, Waves, Willmore City.*
"A Gift," "At a Market in Detroit," "Scar Tissue," "Buds,"
"Clout," "The Cheater," and "Hearing My Daughter Learning
to Read" reprinted by permission of Vesta Publications Limited.

Library of Congress Cataloging in Publication Data

Ditsky, John, 1938-
    Friend & Lover.

    (Ontario Review Press poetry series)
    I. Title. II. Series.
PR9199.3.D517F7   1981   811'.54   80-84832
ISBN 0-86538-011-2   AACR2
ISBN 0-86538-012-0 (pbk.)

Distributed by PERSEA BOOKS, Inc.
225 Lafayette Street
New York, N.Y. 10012

for my parents

CONTENTS

Friend & Lover

HUCK IN HELL

A boy in a cavern on an island
in a storm. He is no longer
alone. It is *all blue-black*
outside, and lovely. It is me
discovering what you contain,
learning to leave the smooth
surfaces of things, to penetrate
to the rough ribbing where real
beauty pulses. The thundering
increases; the wind is whipping
a paradise into a revelation.
He finds out *the pale underside*
of the leaves, the woman beneath
the girl of things. The seed
is surging in its sacs like
lightning. He is grown a man.
You are raining upon the river.

LEMINADE 5¢

If I admire
the cut of your breast
or parade around
in my therefore

you're sure to turn
your sex upside down
fold its metal legs
and be off.

You love to wait
till I'm chin-high
in nice; then,
taking a leg

from the freezer,
you wait for the surge:
the dime on the bed:
the guidon the hoofbeat the horn.

TWO-PART INVENTION

Sudden child napping,
you've been at work
in the garden, now lie
dozing the summer after-
noon away. Above
you, suspended, I'm
taking you in, enjoying
you, savoring. The scent
of sun is on your skin,
smell of earth and green.
Traces of growing things
remind me, awake,
of past loving; asleep,
you cause me dreams
of loving coming. "Assured,"
"certain," swear your legs
in careless sprawling,
say your slack and easy
lips. Tension's not
in you. You're redolent
of past pleasure as a small
town 5 & 10:
candy, cloth and wood:
I taste the coming
moment in the past caught
lightly on your skin.

PONDER, HE SAID

Lady, I
am told to give
no worship to this brief
conspiracy of gristle gland
and fatty tissue that
is you here here
& here, but

I have
seen them sneer
at Chartres leave St. Paul's
yawn at the Florence Duomo and I
reassure you faith and an eye
for art are worth
the having

if having
is a thing you measure
up to. For bare churches,
lady, are all desolate (no matter
how awesome the echo how
lines of vaulting are
bone clean

FLORA

She brings in plants the way
a squirrel hoards against
a bitter day. Flowers

are fingerprints of hers:
she signs the shelves, the sills
in color: *I am here!*

Green things are her book-
marks; they promise a story
soon resumed. She keeps

them wet, the sequence set
and followed as a combination
lock is worked; you've need

of her to get at the goods
inside. Life's her insurance.
Without her, the house would die.

REPAIRING

She is a seamed and parting cell.
The line that runs her body round
conjoins two women! There—
where hair will be if hair
is anywhere—hair's arrowing implies
completion of a zippered whole. Not
so: the bond's impermanent at best,
both brain and body sundered
to polarities of want and will. See:
she's blind along the line, and deaf!

It's touch and taste alone that join
what God has split apart. The proof?
An innuendo of defect. Riddled
with crevice and orifice, the line
at other points descends to speech
—or speaks a braille of vertebrae.
No matter: when allowed, I match
her flaw for flaw, and stay dichotomy
a while: guide sightless tongue to
light, and play that soundless flute.

ROOTING

watering the plant   the water
flowing   the earth bubbling
the plant drinking thirstily
the leaves green and plum
the plant her plant and she
is gone   remembering to water
the watering   remembering
watering the plant   the plant
is leafing new remembering

DEFLOWERING

Oho, she's turned the virgin
once again; fiber and spirit
are grown in spot thought
cleared of obstacle. Effort's
resumed. I wield machete
with a heavy heart: the jungle
lacks restraint. I sigh
in repetition's weariness.

For sharpness is not all,
nor bludgeoning. The honeyed
noun precedes the temporary
verb. A regular attending
keeps the garden in its place
at best: rank chastity,
profuse, hedges my walk;
prune, and it grows the more.

DADDY REMEMBERS

In those days,
I never saw you as
you were. You moved on an axis
of pompon and taffeta; dressed up
in loafers and sweater, white
sox and flaring
skirts, you

were as deep
as wax on a dance floor;
in your mind's yearbook, rhymes
signed you off to *Seventeen*. Inside
my brain, meanwhile, I carried
a matchcover portrait,
miniature

cardboard
gas station calendar,
of someone not at all like you
or anyone: bright favorite slide: all
shiny curves like waxed fruit.
Wax, wax: our plastic
years slid by,

the weekends
we spent kneading each
other like packs of margarine—
a pill within us, pummeled, blushing
the color of synthetic life
through still-intact
sacs. And now

we're moving
in a dreaming dance of years,
humming the old songs, the lies
sustaining lives. It's the last dance
of our senior prom, and we're
facing in different ways,
both staring.

THE NAKED MAN AT THE FIREPLACE

Dying embers, and dying embers.
He is allowed up, by leave, to put
the ashes safe to rest. But the coals
persist, lighting his body as well
as any lover's; the heat shines red
irrelevant on him, like any other.

Speak, someone, of how to turn
his moment to his moment: make some
coal into a lasting light; a flesh
Egyptian, impervious, brown god's.

Hear the wisdom of the naked man:
glowing coals within a darkened room;
this is it and there is nothing more.

THE INCUBUS BEGS TOLERANCE

As groom to very many very briefly, I
would come like Santa Claus down chimneys,
                          or like ghosts
through walls, if I'd capacity. I'd come
                    at night
to lay the gentlest sort of kiss upon the
                    here
and there of many I've admired and had to
                    pass
because extension has its laws. I have
                    this back-
log of remembered graces to reward; it's
                    not
excessive in its length (for both the
                    beauty and
the memory are apt to fade), but long
                    enough
to keep me busy every darkness of the year.
I mean no harm, and wouldn't leave peculiar
                    stains
or progeny behind. But I'd come back re-
                    freshed,
I think, from such nocturnal sending-out
                    of soul,
rejoin my body at your side, and bring you
                    love
all "new and pure" for holding back like
                    what's implied
in white of dresses worn by problematic
                    brides.

THE DECLINE OF COURTLY LOVE

Renunciation is a brick-
and-mortar word. Applied
to two declining adults

in the act of forbearance,
its sound and shape build
cells adjoining churches—

towers to heaven, tombs,
and rooms to view distant
ritual. And you and I

have said politest *Thank
you, no*s to each the other's
mirror-image proffering.

Some other time, perhaps;
some other life. (And *Why
not now?* the small voice

asks—for sin is waste,
but waste is sin indeed.)
Oh no: we'll write us poems

instead, and sing our songs,
like anchorites their vows.
Behold us canonized for love

we ask, each of us holding
stone emblems of virtue
for the other to see across

a nave of time, and standing
snug and frozen in our niches
—rigid, ideal, and pure.

THE ORIENT EXPRESS

This is the train of marriage.
It starts in a green place.

The berth is far too small.

There is a dining car.
There is no dining car.

Someone disobeys the smoking sign.

I am glad to be en route.
I wish I were at home.

Tunnels!

We cross more borders than
we have the visas for.

No one knows how to spell the final stop.

At periodic intervals
I am taken off the train and shot.

HALTING SPEECH

I read Cyrillic and I fracture
French; can find facilities

in Germany and Greece; know
just enough of folkway and odd

song to make a wedding
bearable, an amble worth

the time. I have a stamp
collector's knowledge of Swiss

mail, and fiscal Portuguese.
It's just my English—this

you know—devolves to utter
stutter as I face you past

the pepper and the salt: turns
slur and cipher: semaphore.

PUPIL

Another one has entered in
by eyes, and dwells inside;

another "student," come to teach
herself to me. Another talk

that leaves me feeling touched
as though the talking keyed

an arch that had been building
—leaning pillars, unawares—

through many careful years.
Although I stand before them

naked as a model daily, when
one in hundreds proves to know

my inness like a lover's body—
blush! Another thing like love!

WITHDRAWAL

A *man of consequences,*
someone called him. Meaning
that he'll follow where

his loving leads him, then
pull back, & plead his
duty & *responsibility.*

She doesn't know it yet,
but these his kissings
& his fumbling fondlings

represent the flood-
tide of his surface love.
In time, he'll carefully

explain how X & Y
& Z are all the ways
he might—but won't—

display his feelings on
her person: she already
Xed, & slightly Yed,

and more than ready
for his Zedding. (Wed,
he'll therefore never Zed.)

She peers ahead where
he'd appeared to lead,
instead is faced about

to find he's gone *back*
to Square One where,
she comes to feel, she's

been used, had—& not.
Oh, you're so good,
she smirks: ironic; not.

TAKING OUR TIME

Our love affair has gone on
much too long without

beginning. Regular sight
rubs raw the spot I'd

thought would be appeased
by now, turned comforting

and even special pleasure.
Instead, suspense. Her eyes

speak knowledge, mouth
shows promising; and when

she walks away (she always
walks away, thus far),

the curves of her make
needs to satisfy. Between

the seats of love and lust,
what lies midway, waiting?

She goes, she comes, she goes
—yet seems to circle me

like a fellow wrestler
choosing a hold. Like

moon and sun we are,
seeking a world to light.

SIRENS

A long while since embarking...
Well: hours we floated the river
of night, lying on rugs and couches
by a failing fire, a guttering lamp;

on we sailed, the others asleep
for much of the time, but hearing
still the sound of absent poets
or the last quartets: death's music

both: or the winter waves outside:
death's music too; and finally
I walked my quiet way to bed,
the last to yield to sleep, still

warm with whiskey, knowing in going
candle-in-hand I looked as if
I were in a painting, the beeswax
dripping on my hand as if upon

a catafalque; and now, undressed
in the room that faces water, snow,
my skin shines waxen in the flame.
There is sleep in the house, embers

the fireplace; all is quiet; *All's
well*, save here where I am standing
on the top deck of the ship the house
still listening, lashed to the mast...

A Shining, A Crossing

A GIFT

A freight train is rolling slowly
around this curve in my mind.
The track is rusty; there is
continual screeching. From where
I stand, small in the tall weeds,
I see the brakeman clinging
to the backing-up caboose loom
far above me—then gondolas,
boxcars, last a diesel engine.
Through the scream of strained metal
and the haze of Queen Anne's lace
and milkweed white and green
before my face, I see the fireman
waving dreamily; his hand slides
twenty years aside. Then I reach
upward: Yes: he throws a treasure
downward, whitely plummeting. It is
a piece of thick white railroad
chalk. *What shall I write with it?*

A SHINING, A CROSSING

The sun shining is the sort
abolished since, somehow:
glare off the street palpable
in air. And *I am crossing*

that street, holding the hand
of a young aunt. A shining
everywhere! And is the street
cobbled? There are rails

for streetcars, aren't there?
Before, behind me, stores;
in one of them something
was bought for me, or will

be bought. I clutch or itch
for it. A summer adventure
which continues in a bright
small corner of my brain,

it refuses to turn me loose.
I am crossing that street
still, and when I reach
the curb I will be dead.

BY THE NORTH GATE

We wore white bands
across our chests. Mine

was the furthest oupost
from the school, a corner

where the car plant
traffic passed. In a flat

bleak city, strangely,
one side of me possessed

a house on a hill; the other
a farm. The winds blew

across empty fields; past
me, barbarian lands.

The bells could not be heard.
I passed the children

from the wastes they lived
in; back again.

IN THE COUNTRY OF THE MINES

There was always sunlight in that room. Mornings,
The light crept in from the left, as soon

As the sun cleared the mountain across the street.
You could lie there, thinking about waking,

Your arms reached upwards and back behind
Your head, your hands grasping the round bed

Frame, as you heard the voices from the street rise
Up, the dogs bark, the roosters. The roosters.

When your eyes at last accepted more light
Than the lacy curtains did, you left to play;

But all day long the room kept track
Of the sun's slow glide across the mountain top.

And by late afternoon, though you did not
Know it, how the banked light lingered

In the room long past the setting of the sun.
And some of that light lit your way to bed

Long hours afterward—though you took it
For the glow from street lights. Then when

You fell asleep the last light blew
You out like a wick in beeswax: stood

On guard until you needed more again,
As now. There was always sunlight in that room.

THE PLANES

Back in the days when you played
"Planes" with arms straight out
(instead of swept back), and when
you envied the Zero's compact
shape, the miracle of form of the P-
38, you could stand in fields
and watch the planes go overhead,
flights of planes, squadrons, planes
in armadas catching the sun, the sky
blue, the planes in khaki or dappled
with camouflage, the whole effect
dramatic as war games, clear
as the outlines of glue-backed battle
cut-outs, sharp as the images
on gum cards, colors as vivid
as church art, as post-office
murals: the planes, the planes went
over in hundreds, you could stretch
your neck in those days, we all
looked up then, seeing the planes.

Now the same planes, grounded,
ordered in strict formations, rest
in fields somewhere, the metal torn
and jagged, rusting, the plexiglass
brown and cracked, someone perhaps
much like Dana Andrews still
seeming to sit at the controls, no,
the bombers, fighters, harmless empty
and discarded Christmas toys, do
not make anyone look up now,
their drone sounds only in your mind,
the weeds hold them down, the planes.

THE CHEATER

in the old photograph
                        grandfather
stares
ahead
        the eyes
screened in upon
their own reserve
                        forever

below the white mustache
the mouth is silent

but in the eye
of remember
                twenty years
peel off like plastic death
and the mouth smiles warm

above
        the eyes light white
and sunday
                and there
the lunchpail rests
                        the mines rest
the chicken names herself dinner
(the axe gleams pride
in the woodshed)
                        in the yard
dill and the onion bloom
                                inside
women bustle
                and on his porch
rocker (smiling
                watching)

the foxy card sharp prepares
a swindle of innocent 10

and the bells ring the bells
ring
        down the valley

GRANDFATHER'S CLOCK

Because of Parkinson's disease (the drugs
For it did not as yet exist),

His hand, held out, shook terribly.
(But kindness in the eyes could melt you.)

Black flecks of coal dotted the skin.
(That mine would close, collapse, and soon.)

And when the bad night came, they
Sent me—child—off, out of the way

(A new Red Skelton film had come
To town, to celebrate the health of MG

M). When I got home, the house waved
With wailing women: *Ježiš Maria!* cried

Grandmother (who'd nagged him constantly).
The crying lasted for three days.

Three decades now, and on the bad days,
I hold the hand out, testing tension,

Remembering his hands. (Skelton's nearly
Gone now, like MGM.) No

Coal flecks fleck my hands
(It's Dad's arthritis I expect instead);

Still, I store up sorrow in my gaze
For who will need it, how and when.

RAGE, RAGE

Enfeebled, my father waits for his haircut.
I take the electric clippers, and I place
The plastic guard on top of the metal comb
And do the rough work. I marvel at the way

The grizzled gray curls up while the dark
Lies flat and smooth. It forms a line,
And all I do is follow. With that done,
The guard comes off: it's time for finer

Work. So I work the clippers slowly
Over the ears, where useless comments
Grow; I trim the sideburns; and I shade
The turn from dark to gray in back.

I think I'm done. I ask, and so he rises,
Caneless, grasping the mirror that reveals
My skill, or my ineptitude. And I could weep
At this his vanity, his reaching for the light.

PICTURE OF A MAN, FALLING

Here is the picture of a man,
falling. It has been taken
fast for ease in viewing.

The man doing the viewing
already knows the picture
well, and knows its subject.

So that he feels he knows
the man's expression too:
astonishment, surprise.

So that he's not surprised
at the open mouth of the man
he knows is he, falling.

A STEAL

I think I could still slide into second
(Not that I've played the game in years)

—Imagine me heel-first, spraying dirt,
Slow-motion graceful in a steal, and safe.

(I'd be content to be tagged out: to get
There at all would do.) For these days,

Wonder of which of the first of can-no-
Longer-do events is to occur bedevils me.

(Good thing I do not ski; lucky I've
Never tumbled.) I wait for the mind's fall,

Failing, though—the mental notes all
Suddenly effaced, the mouth mouthing an O.

I think of Renaissance tombs, those last
Slides canceled out and frozen white.

THE KNOWLEDGE OF CHILDREN

We are clothed in the knowledge
of children; they turn our habits
into history, distancing these
our bodies from what are become
our lives. They turn us inside

out, drawing our substances
after them upon their emerging.
Through them, we are unzippered
into dry caricatures—much
like the orange's puckered skin.

KATE IS DANCING

Epitome of sprite,
my naked child dances
before bathing. Her
slim height ignores
sex, anticipates grace.
Her ballet, parodic,
deft, more than mocks
pretense of womanways.

She says: I am;
I will be; This is
my idea of me; You
may wish to take
notes, world. When
this imp hops,
Isadoras clump off.
My heart's her partner.

BUDS

My little girl
takes cheese, sections of sweet
peaches, all on the point of a sharp
knife up to her young mouth;
we, sitting in deck chairs
out in the lakeside sun,
we see only the knife
point and *Ahhh!* our learned
fears in an intake of breath.

My little girl
does not note our astonishment;
content within her browning skin,
she savors flavor that experience
preserves us from. The blade
pays homage to her blood, defers
to self-assurance rich as wine
in her new veins. Life
runs in excess down her chin.

HEARING MY DAUGHTER LEARNING TO READ

Hearing my daughter learning to read
teaching herself by practice—

Trying the spat-out dentals
alongside the shifting vowels:
making words—

I feel pain
as if from deformity's presence
or empathy with a cripple.

Something imperfect
is trying to right itself;

Something hurt
is trying to heal.

The sounds strike me like blows;
their volume, screams.

She is breaking through
(a chick pecks out of its shell):
out of a closed space
into a frightening infinite reach;

Out of a darkness
into a blazing, blazing light
harder to bear than the dark.

She is being born.

INCIDENT

My daughter stopped an assault today
With a knee and a scream. Tears done,
She sleeps upstairs, the more the woman.

And I think of her through the night:
Think of the jug of milk she clutched
Tight trembling—her father's daughter—

Through an alley of time, and brought
Safe home, not a drop of whiteness
Spilled. The bushes and barbed wire

Furl there still, but she's escaped
To bring me the glass of milk I'll drink
In the morning, and a slow rape of wonder.

HOT GOODS

driving daughter & daughter's
friends downtown to high
school   air inside the car
filled up with too much scent
too much makeup too much
yakety-yak   & heat of all this
hothouse forcedbloom toomuch
youngwoman clouds the windows
fore & aft   i peer through
fog hoping to finish delivery
racing the steam   the sprouts
luscious & tender shoots already
springing from the upholstery

PRESENCE

My daughter, you
whom I save from sights
of me that might astonish
or dismay (she claims) by closing
doors, or from the breath

that might appall,
the life that might migrate
and injure, by averting
this my all-too-real
mask, will you

reject me when
this heap of self lies
crumbling—helpless in declining's
final days—as too involving
a presentment;

or, when later
on you share the house
of time with only these chaste
books for father, will
it seem I ever was?

A Voice of Brass

SCAR TISSUE

It runs
nerveless like mapped
rail track. Endowed

with strange strength, its
thick seam protects what
cannot feel, yet seems

set to split along
the line. White
souvenir

of lost whole, it furrows
fallow flesh. *Something
once grew here*, it notes.

THE WAY WE WERE

Look, it's *Breakfast at Tiffany's*!
Eighteen years now, & that cat
is simple skeleton, those shiny
phone booths vandalized ob-
solete & removed; & Hepburn

gorgeous still. (But now it's clear
we'll never make it together.) Even
the powder room costs more,
& nothing lasts but jewels New
York (so to speak) & libraries...

Her name's a poem with one image
only (but it's quite enough); &, like
Moon River, seems in retro-
muse the decade's single joy.
Her face elicits Provençal, & boy.

(Were those lines in her neck
always there? But *quelles* lines,
quel neck!) The feathers float;
alas, the loss, the loss. New
York, & jewelry, & books, & loss...

AT A MARKET IN DETROIT

What are we looking for in here today,
among the people talking in a tongue
we can't begin to cope with? And why

are we wandering among the open olive
casks—so many kinds!—or these
of peppers? These metal cans of oil

and oiled fish that fill the shelves
around us tell us nothing, beyond
a fable of far places. These stone-

shaped breads contain no messages.
Why does the eye linger on the chunk
of white cheese crumbling on a slab

of wood, the knife nearby? We like
our olives jarred, our cheese in plastic
wrap. What are we waiting to hear?

Our houses are outside, among the killers
and hors d'oeuvres. Still we listen,
as if for a signal of struck strings.

DISORIENTATION

1. I am riding my bike at night;
   it's 65, December
   fourteenth. I eat an apple
   and stare at naked houses
   braced for cold that isn't
   there. The breeze comes
   richly from the South: some-
   where down there, James
   Wright puts out the trash,
   and Wendell Berry walks
   the river bank, dressed
   in a nylon jacket; Jim
   Dickey swills his bourbon
   sitting alone on a porch,
   saying *shit*: it is all
   on the breeze. Three miles
   of night Detroit; I head
   for home, surprised, amazed.

2. I sit on my front porch
   smoking a White Owl;
   although I do not smoke,
   the night demands it. (One
   day past, I watched
   a mosquito hatched
   by our winter heat flit,
   crazy, against our window,
   astonished, lost.) The night
   floats up from Tampa,
   from the Gulf, from Cuba, *sí*;
   it is December and I think
   of the men camped by fires
   in the mountains of '58.
   The slow death of yesterdays
   floats like smoke on the air.

3. I write in a roomful of books.
   A poinsettia is in front
   of me, ready to grace
   a frigid feast; it is as red
   as Carmen. Night earth
   is stirring with the crocus
   of misbegotten lusts.
   A gust of thought of woman
   sweeps down from Canada,
   torrid and parched. I head
   for a drink, a phone, a gun,
   for baby Jesus, or a poem.

NIGHT VISITOR

My intruder's always there;
he shares the night with me,
a step beyond the bounds

of vision of my turning head.
He makes his way through walls
and shut doors like a ghost

of substance, means; he slips
inside like a homing cat
and brings my soul a chill

rubbing against its back.
He sits behind me as I
read and, silent, interrupts;

he dictates when I write.
He sends me to my lover's
bed, is there and laughing

by the time I come. And when
I see him finally (I fear
I know), I'll know his face.

PROMISE

A few more of these, and I'll tell
You of being afraid. About being

Scared of going to the store, for fear
Of some rebuff. Of angst over phone

Calls, the nameless stranger selling
You loss. Of even rising in the morning,

The threat of more impingement of out
On in. Or of even waking to the sight

of self in morning's mirror, the fright
You just might fall beyond the frame.

THE TWITTERING MACHINE

The clockwork of dawn is the toy
of God. Time when illusion's

last bats are flitting, are all
that maintains the dead day's dream

to the sleepless eye and brain.
Already cats creep homeward,

footsore furry windup playthings;
and soon the sun will pop up

bubble-swift (the skirted lady
instead of the umbrellaed man).

Gadgets and toys: watch the key
winding (*you see the machinery work*),

the gears a-whirl. At times, the ill-
oiled system squeaks: is birds.

WCW, VA.

"For, Heaven knows why, just as we have lost faith in human inter-
course some random collocation of barns and trees or a haystack and
a waggon presents us with so perfect a symbol of what is unattainable
that we begin the search again."

—Virginia Woolf, *Orlando*

Yes: that is it: the eye's alignment
of the chance in nature: serendipity
of clutter: chicken barrow rain:

the mind's deception of itself: *There's
order here*: the recognition of its own
imprinting: the cards shuffling, sorting

out into a pattern coded to be read
divine: yes: so much depends
upon *So much depends upon* ...

FROM CARMEL COAST

>   "... to feel
> Greatly, and understand greatly, and express greatly,
>   the natural
> Beauty, is the business of poetry."
>   —Robinson Jeffers

One is not up to this: Idea,
it repudiates ideas; poem, it

mocks at poems. It stands up,
rather, as coast rock Ocean

thinks it lessens: as rock,
deceived it survives the waves.

SUCH LOVELY

In this family, nothing is wasted.

I wear a dead man's shirt—
It is my size, exactly. He
Was a leisured priest, maltreated
Rusticated unpromoted by an Irish
Bishopric. (Could pick no Daisy;
Gatsbyed instead in shirts.)

He left me nothing but his blessing,
I presume. And indirectly, this his
Shirt—a leisure shirt. In it,
And mirrored, see me waver between
A blessing (hieratic, sacerdotal)
And the thought of loss, missed chance.

Nothing is wasted in this family.

BLACK & TANS

In nineteen-something, Grandfather
stepped off a boat at the very end
of a line of Irishmen sixty years

long: acquired instantly a set
of asshole ancestors, *forefathers,*
slaveowners moneymen builders

of Taras—which halfass heritage
seventy years of labor improved
to become my portion, lot: a town

where the blood runs in gutters
like rain, history-bound as Belfast.
Adoption triple-locks my doors.

GOING DOWN

Depression, and the end of bitter day,
and you lie staring at the ceiling
of your soul. (The sun takes hours
to go down.) And then, you stand long
minutes in the shower, trying to wash
the stench of failure from your person,
the crust of loss. You're trying to write

a poem of your mood, wanting "concrete
images" for your defeat; they don't come.
(In the old days, they'd have cupped
a vessel filled with heated air
onto your skin—or lanced the flesh
to bleed the poison-humour out...)
Blunt instruments, these pencils, words.

GAUNTLET

Tonight, stalled & searching,
I recall seeing a cat
killed on a road somewhere
—so totally wasted, all
that remained was fur rug
of irregular shape—that,
and a single paw standing
straight up & intact,
warning, waving, or simply
clinging to its own grotesque
integrity: claw poking
memory. I drove it down,
ending the gesture for good.

Nights like these, lessened
to facing how best to say
Nothing to say, the absurd
gray paw returns,
a cheshire admonition,
teasing the mind going
nowhere with the clear threat
of silly end of self:
to last awhile as someone's
stopping place, reduced
to a frail brief erectile
memory, whichever chance
variety a doubtful good.

THE BERRYMAN FLYER

So I'm on the little red wagon,
the Berryman Flyer. The X's on the wall
are drinks not had, to pay for what
good substitute? A traffic ticket?
Anyway, self-conscious as a clever
title, I turn an easy virtue
into a Dead End Kid of words.

Lacking AA arcana,
what chance for freshness? Only
the dry hard poem, hung-
over and bad-breathed, its hand
a-tremble and its liver on the ropes—that
and a snapshot (in his little red
wagon, smiling) of a healthy child.

VACATION

Between the work I cannot, will
not, do and that I can and will
I swing—a child's toy on a string.

Absence of tension's worst of tensions;
leisure relaxes naught. In the still
long dawn of the day away

from "care," there comes a jarring chiding
of the absent, missed alarm: call
of the clear sharp world of *can*...

CHAMBER MUSIC

She pauses in the act of dressing
—having caught sight
of a stranger there in the full-
length mirror. From nearer

on, she finds a fascination
in a body's unfamiliarity,
stares at its bare entirety
closer still: a thrill,

a shock, of non-recognition
shivers her frame; again
she presses forward. More.
At last, she's pressed undressed

full-length against
the glass, loving the self
that scares. Her makeup left
upon the second face, she smiles.

EVENTS

White porcelain
on old linen. Embossed
flowers, the cloth's design, shine
white upon white, but
the white cups

are painted pink
with flowers. Ringed fingers
sort out spoons; the clock tocks
loudly, brown upon the wall.
The dark wooden

chairs are stark
against the papered walls:
more flowers—pink, nearly red—
in oval wreaths of white
on pastel blue.

Tea is poured
steaming. Cream spurts;
in turn, the sugar's taken. Some's
spilled, glittering. There's
time, talk. They

drink their cups
of past together. Out
in the kitchen (except that *this*
is the kitchen) we wait
to read the dregs.

SEND IT BY RAIL

We write. We shunt grief
onto a siding & leave
it there; it rots & rusts

in picturesque decay.
Abandon names the nature
of our art; sidetracked

displays of sorrow never
cause delay. The danger's
that the readiness to switch

by word becomes a habit:
Anticipate in cowardice,
afraid the said word

might derail & spill.
The sadness we're too tied
to fear to risk depletes

our rolling stock; a yard
of empty cars, uncoupled,
tracks a freightless waste.

CLOUT

When the rookies of your youth
retire, & the remembered stars
of back-then are all Hall-
of-Famed & harmless: ink
in the record books: cards
in a pack, rubber-banded,
in the back of a desk drawer,
then yours is new knowledge

of oldness. Though your body
turns up at the training
camp, jogging in place
& chasing the flies of necessity,
your mind has not made
the cut: already, it begs
a job scouting the bushes,
tentative as mud on cleats.

HAMLET AT LUDLOW

This is a play in a ruined
castle. This is a play
in the rain. What if the stage

be filled with corpses? Or
if it's dance-and-song? For
always the castle walls,

always the night—peering
in like the eyes of a skull—
framing the play, mocking

the play, making the play
the All. And what if we stand
offstage and wait and wait

and wait again? What
if we *do* hear applause?
Or not? Or dry on our cue

to die? This is a play
in a ruined castle; this
is a play in the dark.

THE BLACK SHIPS

For miles of Kyushu, we
and the French pair shared

buses: they, moneyed
Boulognais, refused

to condescend to cope
with what I tried to say

their way; instead, a frigid
English was our medium. We

gaped at ginkgo, lotus
and the odd volcano; they

shot footage of the factories
we passed. At Pearl Islands

pier—the Unzen Ferry
waiting—I spoke in irony

about the perfect cloud
above where Nagasaki

was supposed to be; they
talked of the *champignon*

atomique with, no doubt,
the coolest logic. Evenings

they launched out, yukata-
clad, to bathe at every

spa—twelve Cartesian
feet of self-assurance

in the midst of Nipponese
small bustle; we sipped

tea in our room, *pudeur*-
inhibited. And when we

waved an *au revoir*
(that lie) at Fukuoka

station, did they wonder
—as did we—the way

that cultures beg to differ
half a world from home?

THE MARTYRS

Fixed by sex they lie, arrowed
to bed, sheet-staked. In the long
night of this their manic chastity
see how they stare at the bright
white square the light outside
makes on their small cell wall.

The calendar, filled, makes mock.
Joint monks of will, and won't,
they lie by themselves—swearing, bare
—having sworn (but never borne
the like) before. They burn, turn,
on the grill of their faith, never done.

IN DEFENSE OF PROFLIGACY

Regrets. Regrets for the paid-
off mortgage, & the worthless

dollars in the bank. Regrets
for the wines not ordered, &

for every trip deferred. & for
the practical plastic dishes

that will not break, while
crystal cracks, & porcelain

grows crazed. & the love
not gone along with —

prudence, paradigm of death.
Todays left on the plate,

politely, & to waste; & all
the life left for tomorrowing.

A VOICE OF BRASS

—for Wallace Metcalf

In a rock niche in a cold
church floor, & nailed,
I lie. I bear an effigy,

metallic death: life
frozen, stylized, unreal.
I wear a costume & a legend

both: wear has deprived me
of my fine detail. Come
warm me with a paper shroud

awhile; press me with love
& certain care. Your touch
will rub a temporary heat

into my form; I'll leap alive
below your hand. A bit
of brazen me will stay

upon your sheet: a ghostly
souvenir, impressed enough
to stand beside your wall.